Mingled Voices

Proverse Poetry Prize Anthology 2016

Proverse Hong Kong

2017

MINGLED VOICES is an anthology of thirty-one poems, selected from those which were entered in the inaugural annual international competition for the Proverse Poetry Prize (single poems) in 2016.

The Proverse Poetry Prize was jointly founded in 2016 by Dr Gillian Bickley and Dr Verner Bickley MBE, in association with the annual international Proverse Prize for unpublished book-length fiction, non-fiction or poetry, submitted in English, which they also founded in 2008.

Poems could be submitted on any subject or topic chosen by each poet or on the subject chosen for 2016 by the Administrators, "The Environment". There was a free choice of form and style.

Included in the anthology are the poems that won the first, second, and third prizes. Selection to appear in the anthology was also awarded by the judges for the Prize.

The places of birth of the twenty writers whose work is included in the anthology range from Scandinavia to the Far East, to the southern hemisphere; and include Canada, Cap Verde, Cuba, Estonia, Israel, Italy, Macedonia, New Zealand, Norway, the People's Republic of China, Turkey, the UK and the USA. Some have strong links with other countries, including Austria, Chile, Holland, Hong Kong, the Philippines, Spain and the USA.

Mingled Voices

Proverse Poetry Prize Anthology

2016

Contributors

Aytül Akal · Joy Al-Sofi · Maria Elena Blanco

Gili Haimovich · Hei Feng · Akin Jeje · Susan Lavender

Liv Lundberg · Marta Markoska · Mathura (Margus Lattik)

Glória Sofia Varela Monteiro · Keith Nunes

Sam Powney · Vaughan Rapatahana · Angelo Rizzi

Hayley Solomon · Dong Sun · Luisa Ternau

Carter Vance · Mavisel Yener

Editors

Gillian Bickley · Verner Bickley

Proverse Hong Kong

Mingled Voices
International Proverse Poetry Prize Anthology 2016
edited by Gillian Bickley.
1st published in Hong Kong by Proverse Hong Kong, April 2017.
Copyright © Poverse Hong Kong 2017.
Each author retains the copyright in the poem(s)
that appear with their own name(s).
ISBN: 978-988-8228-68-3

Distribution (Hong Kong and worldwide):
The Chinese University Press of Hong Kong,
The Chinese University of Hong Kong,
Shatin, New Territories, Hong Kong SAR.
E-mail: cup-bus@cuhk.edu.hk; Web: www.chineseupress.com

Distribution (United Kingdom):
Christine Penney, Stratford-upon-Avon, Warwickshire CV37 6DN, England.
Email: chrisp@proversepublishing.com

Also available from https://www.createspace.com/6632680

Distribution and other enquiries to:
Proverse Hong Kong, P.O. Box 259, Tung Chung Post Office,
Tung Chung, Lantau Island, NT, Hong Kong SAR, China.
E-mail: proverse@netvigator.com; Web: www.proversepublishing.com

The right of each writer to be identified as the author of the work(s) that appear with
their name(s) has been asserted by them
in accordance with the Copyright, Designs and Patents Act 1988.

Page design by Proverse Hong Kong.
Front cover image by Gillian Bickley. Cover design by Pin-Key Design Co.
Author portraits courtesy the authors and their named photographers.

British Library Cataloguing in Publication Data.
A catalogue record for this book is available
from the British Library.

MESSAGE FROM HASAN ERKEK

When I read this Anthology, I felt that I took a tour in the garden of the poetry world. In that garden each flower has not only her own odour but also has her own shape and meaning. And all flowers were in harmony with each other. I hope one day the real world will be a poetic anthology of humanity, like this.

I congratulate Proverse Hong Kong on the prize, particularly for the anthology.

Hasan Erkek
Turkey

ACKNOWLEDGEMENTS

All those at Proverse Hong Kong, administrators of the Proverse Poetry Prize (single poems), thank all those who entered for the inaugural competition, and warmly appreciate the helpful and willing participation in the editorial process of those whose poems were selected for this anthology.

We are most grateful, also, for the professionalism and dedication of the judges.

Photo acknowledgements for the portraits of poets included in the anthology are due as follows:

Lioz Issac (Gili Haimovich)
Gillian Bickley (Heifeng)
Kaari Saarma (Mathura)
Nikola Adzievski (Marta Markoska).

NOTE FROM THE EDITORS
and Proverse Prize Administrators

For this, the first annual international Proverse Poetry Prize, poems were invited, either on the entrant's own choice of subject or theme, or on a subject selected by the Proverse Poetry Prize Administrators, "the environment" (interpreted as each entrant might wish). Any form, style or genre could be used.

Poems were judged by the panel of judges as submitted and the following awards were made:

First Prize:
Vaughan Rapatahana, 'tin yan don'
Second Prize:
Maria Elena Blanco, 'Temple of Chamundi, Mysore'
Third Prizes:
Joy Al-Sofi, 'White Water';
Gili Haimovich, 'Pedestrians' Cheer';
Luisa Ternau, 'Spring in My Heart'.

Several other entered poems were awarded a place in this Proverse Poetry Prize Anthology 2016, "Mingled Voices", and their names appear in the Table of Contents.

Congratulations to all!

Several of the poems in the Anthology were edited by the writers before publication, but no further judging of the entries was made at this stage.

All writers were invited to contribute a commentary or notes on their poems for this anthology and have responded in different ways.

Brief biographies of each of those whose work is represented in *Mingled Voices* are included in the anthology.

From these, we can see that the writers' places of birth range from Scandinavia to the Far East, to the southern hemisphere; and include Canada, Cap Verde, Cuba, Estonia, Israel, Italy, Macedonia, New Zealand, Norway, the People's Republic of China, Turkey, the UK and the USA. Some have strong links with other countries, including Austria, Chile, Holland, Hong Kong, the Philippines, Spain and the USA.

Entrants were asked to submit their work in English. To qualify, entries needed to be previously unpublished in English, but could have been previously published in another language.

Some of the poems in this anthology were translated into English by the poets themselves (for example, Angelo Rizzi, translating from Italian, and Aytül Akal, translating from Turkish). Some were translated by another person (for example, Hei Feng's poem is translated from Chinese by Dong Sun, who wrote her own poem in English; and Liv Lundberg's poem was translated from Norwegian by Susan S. Senstad).

Among those who wrote directly in English are several for whom English is not their first or mother-tongue. These writers include Marta Markoska, Mathura (Margus Lattik), Glória Sofia Varela Monteiro, Vaughan Rapatahana, Dong Sun and Luisa Ternau.

Maria Elena Blanco is a special case. She wrote her poem, 'Reversible Fields' in English and later translated it into Spanish. As far as she remembers, her other poems included here she wrote in Spanish and translated into English.

Some of the poets have elaborated on their knowledge and use of various languages.

Angelo Rizzi explains that, although his mother-tongue is Italian, he wrote his first poem in Arabic (he has a *Licence en Language, Culture and Arabic Literature*). Later, he began to write poems in Spanish and in recent years, he has written in Italian.

Luisa Ternau writes, "I wrote all the entered poems in English. I fell in love with the English language as a teenager. I cannot remember how it happened. I think it must have been because of some poems or some story that was part of the English curriculum. My native language is Italian. Also, I have always spoken Trieste's dialect fluently. I love writing in English. Most of my writing is in English. Also, I think that my public is more international than Italian. In the past I studied German, Spanish, Japanese and Chinese."

Maria Elena Blanco, whose mother tongue is Spanish, has also used English as a main language for many years, also speaking French fluently. She has studied Italian and German as well. For the past thirty years and continuing she has worked as a translator (from English and French into Spanish) for the United Nations.

Several of the poets are also translators of work by other people.

Some of the writers whose work appears in "Mingled Voices" are already well-published as poets, whether in magazines and journals or in book form. Among them are prize-winning writers and writers who have participated in poetry festivals and other prestigious events. For at least one writer, on the other hand, this is her first published poem. For some, poetry is only one of the literary genres that they write in.

Most writers chose to enter a poem on a subject or theme of their own choice although some did focus on the subject selected for this inaugural competition by the Proverse Poetry Prize Administrators, "the environment". Each poem was judged on its own merits and those selected for this anthology are arranged simply by title. Poems written for children are given a section of their own. The poets' commentaries and notes on their poems, requested during the editing process, are presented as endnotes. The brief biographies of the poets (which were not known to the judges at the time of judging) appear in alphabetical order of poets' surnames.

Poems were invited in any genre or style. Most are in free verse. But Vaughan Rapatahana entered two poems in his particular style of concrete poetry and Maria Elena Blanco also entered one poem where the shape of the words on the page echoes the title and content. Hayley Solomon is unique in this collection for her use of strong rhythm and rhyme.

THE PROVERSE POETRY PRIZE 2017

We very much hope that all who entered for the inaugural international Proverse Poetry Prize and all whose poems are included here will continue to enter their work in future years. And of course we hope that others will join the competition in 2017.

Receipt of entries for the 2017 competition begins on 7 May 2017 with 14 July 2017 as the deadline.

As in 2016, poets may enter poems either on a subject or theme of their own choice or on the theme suggested by the Administrators for 2017, "Happiness", interpreted as each poet may wish. Full and updated details will always be available on the Proverse website, proversepublishing.com.

In the meantime, we hope those whose poems are included in the 2016 Proverse Poetry Prize Anthology will enjoy seeing their and others' work and that all their readers will share the pleasure of the judges and the editors in these "Mingled Voices".

Gillian Bickley and Verner Bickley
Hong Kong

PREFACE

The invitation to writers of poetry to enter the new competition, inaugurated by the founders of the Proverse Prize, has happily appealed to writers in many countries. Readers will be grateful that those for whom English is not their mother tongue have generously been willing to create work in English or translate it or have it translated into English, so making it even more widely accessible than it already is in their mother tongues.

One stipulation for entry to the competition was brevity and the poets represented here have responded with some very pleasing cameos. Other terms of reference offered a wide choice: although The Environment was suggested as a starting point, writers were also invited to include reflections on any theme or experience. Some did so. Maria Elena Blanco, for instance, responded with images from the great rivers and temples of India where the senses are assaulted by the vibrant colour and intensity of the rituals and ceremonies performed by devotees. It is not merely vivid scenes that she recollects but the realization of something deeper: exuberant life sits easily with the rituals accompanying death on the 'All Purpose' sacred river.

The changes in our environment, not all of them man-made, concern the inhabitants of every country on earth, and it is refreshing to see the response from writers in so many lands. Vaughan Rapatahana's narrator looks down from his high window to see the small figure almost obscured by the smog in the canyons of Hong Kong's cityscape – a homunculus, a smitten manikin; in another continent Joy Al-Sofi contemplates the plight of the mother bear with her cubs waiting for the salmon that may never return; the sight of a submerged Lycian city prompts Aytül Akal to think of a child who lived there hundreds of years ago and to imagine his surprise if he could now look down from the boat that floats over his old home in the depths below.

The pleasure of reading poetry is enhanced by a glimpse of the occasion that triggered a particular response. In this anthology we have the benefit of the writers' own illuminating commentaries on their poems. Through their own words we are able to discern the genesis of a poem in the experience that prompted the writer to record some significant event or scene. My feeling is that the reader of this selection of poems will be impelled to turn back from the writer's commentary to read the poem again and perhaps be rewarded by a glimpse of some extra subtlety in thought or form.

Margaret Clarke
Oxfordshire, UK

CONTENTS

POEMS

A Metropolitan Vision[1]
Luisa Ternau

A crowd of skyscrapers competes,
Each one hoping to reach the clouds.
Down in the playgrounds,
Students play basketball, their arms lifted,
Girls chase a tiny tennis ball,
Children take part in speech contests.
It's all about who's the best, the fastest, the ablest.
Hey! Can you say the ablest?
Until our own sun moves beyond the horizon,
behind an orangey-red curtain,
Only then it will make sense – maybe –
all this running after dreams
as thin as the sound of words,
as solid as a tennis ball,
as large as a palace,
as candid as cheerful clouds
on a sunny day.

Abandoned To Their Pleasure, Khajuraho[2]
Maria Elena Blanco

If you enter the space that the Lady of the Unicorn opens
within you,
(…) you will experience a strange pleasure; a newly-found
freedom will
rise in your gestures. (…) Perhaps you will even have the
revelation of
a kind of desire which lacks nothing.
    Yannick Haenel
    À mon seul désir

What woman has not bent down to remove a thorn
from her foot while naked or scantily clad with veils
or bangles, in the twirls of love or dance, or simply
when making up her eyes in front of a low mirror.

But we are here in the tenth century and Hemavati
has been raped by a god, gives birth to a prince
amidst a forest of high date palms, vows
to build the architecture of desire.

(In the fifteenth another Lady locks her body
with a red velvet key and secretes a mute passion
through the five orifices from her garden in bloom.)

And so these tough females on proud islands
are like our twenty-first century gals
with their tangas and silicone tits.

(Or else they are the Lady and I, entranced
in heraldic bliss.)

As on the indigo carpet, the scene
evolves outside, the enigma deep down,
visible only from the rear eye, in the cold-sweat
cavity of the stone or skin-lined temple.

Abandoned to their pleasure, the libertines
gathered in those sand-swept times
somersault into the void.

All-Purpose River, Varanasi[3]
Maria Elena Blanco

J'ai plus de souvenirs que si j'avais mille ans.
    Charles Baudelaire

Here one becomes eternal in twenty-four hours.

The air is like an ashen, aromatic gunpowder
delving into each wrinkle and the slightest
of gestures tips the balance of karma.
In these same waters, where one washes or burns
sour chocolate bodies draped in saffron
or turquoise, floats a flaming red sari
conveniently recouped from the pyre,
a no-hit in the eyes of the holier.
Seven gurus consume the daily twilight
with rituals of fire and since the break of dawn
the young apprentice yogis do headstands
on the steps while an enlightened swami
voices his silent prayer *urbi et orbi.*
All the colours and liquids nose-dive
into the Ganges. A striding bull
holds court under a shed and Shiva's
flying bull reigns on the altars.
Throngs of tourists gradually grow pale
until they disappear amid spiritualities
firmly versed in nothingness. It is difficult,
very difficult to separate in Varanasi
the smoke from the shadows,
the void from the fear of the void.

Atlantic[4]
Liv Lundberg

Translated from Norwegian by Susan S. Senstad

I am *muntu* – a human being –
my feet are not planted on earth
my roots grow upwards
nourished by air and by light

I ram the North Cape
into the Atlantic body
and am pulled by
the Caribbean desire
that brings life
to this hostile coast

I follow the Atlantic cable
through ocean-dark depths
from the Arctic ice
to Tierra del Fuego's lights
across open green island eyes

I braid the Aurora sisters
into the lattice of star writing
above my sea charts
to navigate from North Cape
to the Cape of Good Hope

A hope out of the ocean
against the history of atrocities
of the Rainbow Nation that
sorted and separated its tribes

I touch the scars – the fault lines

What kind of man are you?
the victim asks his torturer
during the Truth and Reconciliation
Hearings and receives the reply:
I ask myself the same question

Were I a human being
I would stretch out my arms
and take a piece of the rainbow – *Kwammang-a* –
a member of the San people's sacred
family of insects and animals

I would give the human being
that piece of rainbow
I would give the rainbow a world
and I would give the world a human being

(Else)Where?[5]
Marta Markoska

In the desert of my soul
stop thinking of vanity
refuse thinking of vanishing
decline thinking of serenity
I think how peace means emptiness

Nothing is more blessed than living in nothingness
No one has the right to break the spontaneity
Neither knowing how to forget, nor how to forgive

We are doing no more than playing in a one-act play
Naïve is everyone who thinks doing better is forcing things
to happen
Navigating towards self-glorification, neglecting others,
We are no more than a drowning man catching a straw.

Finding peace in nothingness is possible
– no one ever lived there!
Finding tranquility in emptiness is certain
– nothing ever disturbed its essence!
(Not even this exclamation mark)

Escape From Absolution[6]
Keith Nunes

shootings of light pierce the dark
on the path where warriors
scurried ahead of mobilised armies;
where leaves are trampled three centuries below
and arching rivers grind against yielding soil

a tomblike silence
quells and evokes fear in the same breath
a pulsating stillness
that is vanquished with a footfall
or scream

a bird that has its name tattooed
on the inside of my eyelids
speaks hesitantly
among rivals and
scheming predators

there's no excuse;
no mercy
it's the aftermath of the revolution
and those who hang
look down with pity on those who live

you came with divine hope
but leave timid, unadorned
dragging ancestors' debts,
hiding rough-hewn scars,
pleading with passing motorists

"save me"

Hues of the Storm[7]
Akin Jeje

Mong Kok, Tuesday night, a crash from the smog,
A splintering of china plates,
And it has only just begun to roar.

Dark colours, ashen and slate,

A fresh shower of rain, a little pain,
Solitary, grey-knit middle-aged woman,
Weeping on a crowded train.

Deep colours, violet and agate,

Steady torrent of splashing streaks, unbounded by joy,
Couple's sealed bright lips at MTR Yau Ma Tei,
Jaded eyes dart from throngs, knowing but coy,
To add to hues of the storm.

Setting colours, sapphire and loam,

Aftermath of the evening's relentless downpour
Leaves bellies sated, eyes bedazzled by neon slashes and
chops and hordes and shops,
Deaf from the cacophony of bass to razor-soprano tones on
a million mobile phones,
Concrete still tinkles and sparkles with the last refrain of
the night's fallen rain.

But it's time, before the indigo-cloak, the Pearl Delta
smoke appears, time to go home.

It's time, before the colours blur into soaking eyes, ashen
and slate, violet and agate,
Indigo, sapphire and loam.

It's time it's time, before the peerless sky disintegrates into
discoloured dreary foam,

That's no longer filtered, just veiled and cold. It's time to
go home.

Intertexting in India[8]
Maria Elena Blanco

On the occasion of Miguel Hernández's centenary,
1910-2010

To Ranjit Hoskoté

I run into Miguel Hernández in India
in the lines of Mumbai poet Hoskoté
– a forward flight since it is he who
comes to me though it was I, elusive,
who was at fault and had to find him.
'Corrida' is the poem the Indian dedicates
to him in English, I read it with the nervous
pleasure of a tantalized palate, already
savouring the mix of blood and water,
sand and dust, bull and minotaur
in the decomposed red, male-borne fatality,
frothy crossing which rips the metaphor
with the voracity of the hollow womb
of goddess Hunger, the one who sucked
my breath away at Khajuraho.
I smell the Mediterranean in the Arabian Sea,
and then the Andalusian moon appears
over the Ganges, perfumed with votive
incense and roses from the funeral fires.
All of Hernández's moons – rhetorical,
Moorish, moistly iridescent with sequins
or dew – I had ignored in favour of
the olive growers sung by friendly voices,
an image that would only take hold in the flesh
as I was lost in the green sea of Jaén.

Moveable topics, bull and moon, which
like desire displace it all in their wake,
leaving ochre-red ashes and white blood
on the gray mantle of sky, sea or page,
digging into what strives to surface and
finally emerges where it was least expected.
I learn to know Hoskoté and to unlearn
Miguel, I learn to know myself and process
the three of us in this intertextual grinder
which exceeds us in its potential, its defeat.
I hear Miguel Hernández with my third eye,
reopen Hoskoté with one ear to the West,
mentally recall the path that brought me here:
Andean, tropical, structuralist, baroque.

It is never too late to do poetic hara-kiri.
It is always too late to learn to know a poet.

Light Of Bones[9]
Margus Lattik (Mathura)

To Pär Hansson

You know that summer will come
and spread its deceptive warmth all over the shadows;
you know that rye will come up in the fields
and suffer drought after drought for your lack of desire.

In order to be alive,
you need to walk out on the open field above the heaven's
valley
and scythe your self-awareness
with a single strike.

In order to write,
you need to go back to the house where hay grows
in through the windows,
wind flutters the mouldy curtains
and cracks in the floorboards
let the coolness of your spirit's den seep in.

Slowly, you crawl out
of the stinking quagmire of welfare
and feel your bones go on growing,
growing inwards, filling with light.

My Typical Day[10]
Dong Sun

The sun is
most brilliant
when defeated.
Smog lifts my cheeks,
flowerpox in the flower basket,
chickenpox in the wok.
All is well.

The world is yours.
You are monstrous,
Old Beetles,
digging your vast swamp,
smoking your high weed.

The world is not ours.
We are little befuddled creatures,
breathing our little graves,
harvesting our little tobacco hearts.

In the smog, a haze of splendour,
Bitter ocean and rosy lips are
indulging and reprimanding,
fragmented, shallow and light, all here.
All is well.

Night Is Still Firing Guns[11]
Hei Feng

Translated by Dong Sun

This is some frightened flesh this is
Some bitter flesh this is
Some singing flesh this is
Some flesh flying in the sky

But
One sack
How much cruelty and patience it costs

Full of bullet holes, the sky is dimming
There, guns go on shooting
The muzzles of guns keep searching…
Soon, the sky turns from dark to black
– before noon
Human midnight is here

When birds flutter away
All the spines in the sky fall on the ground
Bullets first pierce
the conscience of the sky
then penetrate our lungs
through birds' nests clocks music notes…
before they stab our souls
and pass through our ancestors
Something most treasured is perhaps our finality falling
Medusa's head is soon to arise

Bang bang bang bang…
Night is still firing guns

Once Grown, Now Gone, and Green No More...
Ode to the Environment and Our Planet
Hayley Solomon[12]

Lest the earth grow warm beneath my feet and summer
solstice turn to heat,
lest rhythms of the greenhouse sun bear down on me, the
sated one –
sated with a life replete, dappled by swift pleasures' mete,
too quick to care, the air replete with factory fumes and
fossils' sleet,
lest the earth grow warm and cooling ice like ribboned
rivers
carve and dice our planet earth not once, but thrice,
from north to south the polar ice, and searing rains on forest
floor –
the stumps of trees,
once grown,
now gone,
and green no more.

Oh, yes:
It's water's rage and waves of ice
that drown,
then drain,
in eon's trice.
Lest no one listen, I will, wind,
I'll sing your song and caution bring.
Come beckon fire, earth and air, I'll touch with care
your free fruits fair.
And, plucking fruits,
I will allay
the wild of winds and plant, I say,
the seeds for hope for morrow day – from sapling tall to
caraway.

I will not take without true need.
nor need so much I turn to greed.
The earth's small hints are mine to read,
so heed I will –
I will indeed.

Pedestrians' Cheer[13]
Gili Haimovich

We, the pedestrians, are of a different caste.
In urban scenery, among the humans,
ours is the closest to animal nature.
Much heavier than birds,
and much rarer,
we migrate from one side of the pavement to the other.
We're the only species that gathers in random flocks,
even just to cross the road, supporting one another,
standing by a traffic light.
Come humid heat wave or polar plunge,
we become single, singular and less,
just like the birds, in need of breaking free from cages,
but out and about;
even if what is out there
that we're so keen about
is as ambiguous.
We turn each bus seat, every subway car,
into a temporary nest, a home,
even though public.
You'll recognize us,
the only ones comfortable biting a sandwich on the move.
Watch our legs,
salute the changing seasons reflected
on our skin, our faces.
When we come to your homes, oases,
respect us
the same way you'd honor a truth-telling mirror.

You, air conditioned-people,
soon the planet will be solely yours.
We'll be extinct,
no better than any other breed,
we, the pedestrians, with all modesty, the servants of
modern lives.
For what is a main street, main stream, mainstream
without its sides, its sidewalks, and its side walkers.

Plastic Soul Recycling[14]
Luisa Ternau

In the lonely graveyard,
where visitors can rarely come,
it is better to bring
plastic flowers to console the souls
of those people of long ago;
Because live flowers
are always eaten by the wild goats
roaming the open countryside.

I was told that plastic things
cannot hold a soul in them;
and yet as a child
I expected all my dolls to have a soul.

Girlfriends are convinced that
the soul of love hides only in live flowers,
and blame their boyfriends
for their gift of plastic roses, bought
(as the jealous seller puts it), because,
"They never fade:
the best way to express your unfailing love, Sir".

Plastic is recyclable:
What about the soul of its objects?

Once their life ends,
natural things get recycled also,
slowly and imperceptively,
while their souls wander wide and long,
waiting to be free from any shape –
or maybe already feasting
in their new status...
And the souls of plastic objects follow too

Psalm[15]
Joy Al-Sofi

By the rivers of Babylon,
Where I lay down
And there I wept when I remembered
Green pastures of plenty and
Still waters that once ran clear.

Help me, O Lord, God of our salvation!
For I have lost my way.
Riversides where birds once layed
Are now but feathered graves.
Return to me mine inheritance.
Save me from the ditch of mine own making.

Everything that breathes now sings,
Give praise unto the Lord!
For in the day when once I cried,
Thou filled my cup with milk with honey
And didst deliver me.

Thy waves and billows red-slicked ride,
Unloosed on a poisoned tide.
I lift up mine eyes unto thee, O Lord:
Wilt thou be angry with us forever?
Let not the waters overthrow me.
Save me with thy deliverance!

Anoint with oil thy troubled waters,
Cleave them from dry land.
Make haste! Let them not conjoin the earth
For the waters have come in unto my soul.

My cup runneth over.
Surely goodness and

I cannot breathe
Mercy!

Rain[16]
Glória Sofia Varela Monteiro

Translated by Candida Mendes

The sun throws its sharp rays
At the earthly body
As a knife opens wounds,
Denuding the poor soil soul.
They open the vent of the clouds
In the hands of the winds,
Drop the colourless life
With a net tenderness.
There is dancing life in the air.
With the eyes of the speed
Losing life
She comes with light
A melancholy bright
Falling in the depleted fields,
Burning the sun's arms
Creating hopes
Breaking the heat anguish
Dragging bitterness flood
Taking everything to the ocean,
The rain arrives cultivating
Love in the different faces.

Reversible Fields[17]
Maria Elena Blanco

To Anne Waldman

Looking in a mirror in broad daylight, a woman
sees herself threefold: she whose hair
is being coiffed, she who handles
the hair, she who holds the
mirror, bejeweled, clad
in colour, protected by
the sun-lit scene.

Looking in a
mirror in the depth of night,
a woman sees her absence and
the candle that will light her deathbed. Off
the jewelry, off the tight corset, the lace petticoat.
In the chiaroscuro she has already lost her lower half, sits
on her darkness, her black hair soon accomplishing the rest.

Smoker's Cough[18]
Carter Vance

I light up, snuff out, the candle,
wax burning down both ends of it,
for the finger-running freedom of
what it is to wait for minute-days
at the crooked station staircase at Pancras,
swell of wrought summer iron,
bar gates construction, post-war tile.
When we met, my skin was
cigarette cellophane, giving thin
cover to toxicity, rapping brush
of shore wave carrying crescent moon tide;
I could have washed the old person away.
But you saw through, past the packet
street litter in August rain,
to be so clutching, unadorned
washing out each other's colours
to bleached brown PoMo
in train car light.

Special Objects[19]
Maria Elena Blanco

Nature's bounty, stuff of dreams:
earth caught in eucalyptus jug, air
trapped in wings of laughter,
smells of incense, herbs,
oozing from sultry skin
and soft fake nails.
    Dog barking, chit-chat,
horror interrupt the gift of love
or art: timeless amber
in Umbria, wrapping up
a poem in Capri.
        Gifts
one doesn't know who gave
or who's receiving:
fantasies, flaws, false starts
teach us patience to listen,
trust in craft, hope
of fulfillment.

Spring In My Heart[20]
Luisa Ternau

Spring in my heart,
Spring everywhere!

Imposed on myself
Like artificial snow
On the Alps
When the tourist season
Is on.

The time for blooming
Will also come,
With flowers growing on the slopes,
Uncontemplated by the ski-ing crowds.

Spring will be only for the moon
And for the stars;
Blossoms remaining
Unnoticed
on the deserted ski run.

Sunny Spratly Parasols[21]
Sam Powney

Does the ocean wave?
Dark unsettled tarpaulin –
grey swathes twitch taut, sharp gold glints.

The sun has got his hat on – is he
coming out to play?
Exhausted air-con drips,
a melded shirtman steams.

Do the hills rejoice?
Silent monochrome humps.
Wisps of cloud hiss, disappear.

Was the storm a blast?
Ice branches in summer sky,
sudden dumbstruck black-out blocks.

Which land owns the rocks?
They mewl to the eastern sea.
In giant plastic gyres
her belly starts to heave.

Temple of Chamundi, Mysore[22]
Elena Maria Blanco

The monkeys are a consolation for the bull I missed
below, at the foot of a staircase made for sinners.
Instead, the rickshaw dragged me all the way to the top
as the sun plunged down in glory, stumped
by smog. The goddess did not deign appear,
only her untouchable servants may woo her
amidst a rolling kitchen of minced roses,
paste of shredded petals, cardamom cream,
in the underworld of her *sancta sanctorum*.
We mortals, surfing along corridors, spot
stone counters, chamber pots, basins
tinted with red and yellow, peaceful *teocallis*
meant to cut off flowers, not heads. Even the cows
wish to visit Chamundi, who is feasting
her birthday. One of them boarded the bus,
where the revered one's photograph was posted
under garlands of marigolds and the driver
did everything to lead us to our death.
What would we find in Chamundi's overcrowded
heaven? Perhaps the airy, simple, unscathed,
incorruptible secret of the void.

The 69 Club[23]
Susan Lavender

The fighter generation
Was born in the wake of the First World War,
Suffered hunger and the Depression,
Spent their heyday fighting – and believing in – the Second
    World War.
They lived frugally in austerity and remained strong.

Their sons and daughters instead were hippies, flower
children,
Embracing peace, rejecting their parents' war as wrong.
They lived hedonistic lives to the full – perhaps to excess?
Making love not war, with wine, weed and song.

Their heyday was '69's Summer of Love
Three days of Peace and Music (as well as Love)
Under the symbol of the Dove.

Old soldiers never die
But flowers quickly fade;
So goodbye Bowie, Rickman and Frey.
The hippies who blossomed in '69
Are withering now, around sixty-nine;

But soldiers who survived under war's bitter bond
Continue to live, into their nineties and beyond;
Their flower children falter and die before them.

Now we, the hippies, are leaving.
So we salute you, the "Y-Gen,"
Your future now looms.
We entrust to you our soldier parents,
grieving
for us, the "Flower-Gen".
Flowers cannot bloom
in this century's fumes.

The Essential[24]
Angelo Rizzi

this disordered world
has a bad reputation;
but the poet intervenes,
recognizes the chaos,
does not make a drama
indeed he mitigates,
sums it up,
in the essential's language.

the rain[25]
Vaughan Rapatahana

the rain leers in
        my window
like a dirty old man.

he lurks
most of the morning,
skulking
a r o u n d
the roof
ratatapping the doors
        &
daring me to exit.

when I do,
I am the doppelganger –
the slashed raincoat,
my gauche hat,
an umbrella obscenely
        gnarled b e y o n d redemption,

        &
a permanent louche squint –
his teeming tears cannot conceal.

tin yan don[26]
Vaughan Rapatahana

I swear I saw him again –
yesterday, it was –
deep d

       o

         w

           n

f r o m   my 30th floor windows,
cresting high in
tin yan estate.

churning his arms circulatory,
yes, rather like some
lilliputian windmill,
he air-strode
an errant *tai chi.*

he seemed to be chanting something,
but what could I decipher
from my own aerial roost?
he was homunculus to me.

this morning, giving up trying
to spy shenzhen
through the perennial glutinous pall,
I plodded home,
across the motley square,
replete with cheap lots,
haggled
        at the local market.

there he was once more,
    spindly beneath
a w i d e s c r e e n hat;

this time motionless,
staring silent a c r o s s the nullah
like some smitten manikin.

'jóusàhn', I smiled, twice it was
'lei hoi m hoi sam?'

he maybe blinked; offered nothing in return –
except a flourish
of the plastic fan
he always stowed
inside a timeworn tunic
three times the size of him;
fixated in some quixotic quest,
only he could fathom.

yet,
his riposte captured me
                                        two metres   further   on,
about to key the entrance code.

'siempre', it was,
gifted through his skinny whiskers.

nothing more.
'siempre', only.

'siempre',

indeed.

[*jóusàhn* – Cantonese – good morning
lei hoi m hoi sam? – Cantonese – are you happy?
siempre – Spanish to Tagalog – always]

White Water[27]
Joy Al-Sofi

Mother bear's alone with cubs
at riverside.
The drop at the falls is half what it was.
Foaming white water
where salmon and bears collect
is now neck-deep and empty.

Much effort to brace against
the wake of
the crazed, unstoppable current.
Perhaps the rest have tired,
eaten enough, taken a chance
to hone up on hibernation skills.

Bears will waken and return.
These spawning salmon
will not.
Soon the summer run will end.
Rivers flow without end.
Does the river hibernate in the sea?
Does it rest in the deeps
till it's time to rise again?

Will the seas rise?
Will bears wake in winter dark?
Will the Pacific circle of salmon
come round again?
Will we know when we've seen
the last one?
Will the ice melt?

Will we wake up alone?

Will we
Wake up

Winter Garden[28]
Maria Elena Blanco

...long, corner-squeezed houses infinitely watching the
trains go by...
    Jorge Luis Borges, 'The South'

To Hillary Keel

Sitting in the winter garden, I take the keys,
put on my boots to go out in the snow
and head back to the city.
Outside, the backyard is a milky sheet
cut across by nightly shadows and the shimmer
of a lamp post, the greenery provided
by the interior rubber trees and cactuses
and the whitish pines stepping in
through the high clear walls.
Suddenly, in the dark silence, the tram,
the last one, skims just past the glass pane
and sends me reeling from country to country, to the ranch,
the hospital, the blow
on the staircase with the open leaf,
and from there to the classroom,
the professor now dead
and the book I still owe him,
the streets of my childhood and that other
windowed staircase,
to my South of souths,
the souths of my
South.

Fortunately, Hillary, you found
the car keys in the winter garden.
Thanks for the evening, thanks
for the magic
of your home.

POEMS FOR CHILDREN

A Boat on the House[29]
Aytül Akal

Translated into English by Aytül Akal

Hundreds and thousands of years ago
The child who lived in this house
Did he ever imagine just like us,
>Talking to his toys,
>Flying to the clouds,
>And writing stories
>On the windows?

Hundreds and thousands of years ago
The child who lived in this house
Did he ever dream, just like us,
>Diving into the ocean,
>>Walking on the Moon,
>>Flying to the Stars?

Like all children,
He surely imagined
The furthest supernatural
And the craziest dreams.

However
Hundreds and thousands of years ago
The child who lived in the city
Now sunk deep under the sea,
Never thought
In hundreds and thousands of years,
That a boat would float
on his wrecked house.

The Mountain and the Sea[30]
Aytül Akal

Translated into English by Aytül Akal

Down the mountain kneeled,
Before the beautiful sea.
The scent of a bunch of thyme
It gave to its sweetie.
Day after day told its love
That will ever be.

Each time they embraced,
A piece of themselves
In love they exchanged.

The mountain piece by piece
Slipped into the sea.
The sea piece by piece
Turned into a mountain.

Down the mountain kneeled
Before the beautiful sea...

Questions to the Rock[31]
Aytül Akal & Mavisel Yener

Translated into English by Aytül Akal

Talk to me rock!
Once upon a time
Were there
Children on Earth?
Did they ask you
Millions of questions too?

Tell me rock,
Why are there on Earth
So many shades of colours,
So many different breeds?

What if there were
No blue, no red, no pink,
No shade on anything?
What if there were
No trees, no birds, no species?
No cultures, no mankind, no races?
No civilizations?

Hey silent rock!
I don't think you're dumb!
One by one, and slowly,
You tell all the mystery
All the drama of history

So many children have been born
So many lived and are gone.

Hey friendly rock!
Take my greeting in all languages;
Carry it forward
Thousands of years away.
Tell the children there that,
Thousands of years ago,
A child both like and unlike them
Asked questions of you too.

NON-ENTERED POEM

Intimates
Gillian Bickley

On the way from Mother Teresa Airport to the centre of
Tirana, Albania, 17 October 2010.

The strip of grass,
dividing the airport road,
had enough to offer a meal to a cow;

– and there was the cow, grazing;

and at her side, squatting down
intimately and familiarly,
was her owner,
his stick across his knees,
close to her,
looking at her,
talking to her:

"Now, Daisy,
you fill yourself up; you make a good meal.
I'll just squat here,
next to you,
keeping you company,
till you're done."

It was exciting to see
such familiarity
between man and beast;
the good relations we ought to have;
which we remember from our childhoods past
– or the childhoods we should have had, but never did –
and that our futures never can retrieve.

And we traveling people, flying here and there,
in and out of countries,
watching news on television
of the species, that are dangerously close to death,
Is there anything we do, but regret?

Will we change one iota of what we do,
day by day, to mitigate the causes,
accumulating towards such a loss?

"As flies to wanton boys are we to the gods;
They kill us for their sport." So Shakespeare wrote.

The human species acts thus too.

Maybe we cannot escape our own extinction
in due course. – "Those whom the gods
wish to destroy, they first make mad." –

But until then, let us act like gods
ourselves; and save those species that we can.

From *Perceptions*, Proverse Hong Kong, 2012.

POETS' BRIEF BIOGRAPHIES

(Based on Information Supplied by the Poets)

Aytül AKAL
(b. İzmir, Turkey, 1952) dreamed of being a writer since her childhood.

For many years, from 1974 onwards, she worked as a journalist for magazines and newspapers.

She now has more than 150 books for children and young adults published in Turkey and over fifty books published abroad in German, Spanish, Hungarian, Arabic, Persian, English, Bulgarian, etc.

In 2010, she was nominated to represent Turkey for the International ALMA Award (Astrid Lindgren Memorial Award). In 2012, her books were the subject of research presentations by academics at a three-day symposium held at Eskisehir Osmangazi University, Turkey.

Her poems and stories have been published in school textbooks. She writes stories, fairy tales, picture books, novels, poems and plays. She is also building social projects aiming to promote reading culture and personal development in children.

She has won several prizes for her books and for her devotion to children's books.

Joy C. AL-SOFI is a published writer of poetry, fiction and nonfiction.

Originally from the USA, she has been teaching English in Hong Kong since 2004.

Maria Elena BLANCO
(b. Havana, Cuba, 1947).
Poet, essayist, translator.

She writes mostly in Spanish and translates her own work into English.

She has worked as a university professor and researcher, and is a translator for the United Nations.

Her books of poetry include *Posesión por pérdida* (1990), *Alquímica memoria* (2001), *Mitologuías: Homenaje a Matta* (2001), the English chapbooks *Vestal Myths/Solstice Fires* and *Felix Austria/Reality Fireworks* (2001 and 2004, respectively), *danubiomediterráneo/ mittelmeerdonau* (2005), *Wilde Lohe* (in German translation, 2007), *El amor incontable* (2008), the bilingual anthology *Havanity/Habanidad* (2010), *Escrito en lenguas* (2015) and *Sobresalto al vacío* (2015), as well as two essay collections, *Asedios al texto literario* (1999, literary analyses) and *Devoraciones. Ensayos de período especial* (2016, Cuban cultural studies) and translations of Austrian poets.

Besides English, her own poetry has been translated into German, French, Italian, Romanian and Hindi.

Her work is represented in many poetry anthologies and has been awarded, among others, the prize, La Porte des Poètes (Paris, 1996) and the Grand International Prize for Poetry of the Academy Orient-Occident (Romania, 2016). She divides her time between her homes in Vienna, Santiago de Chile and the Andalusian countryside.

Mr Hei FENG is a poet, fiction writer, essay writer and the editor of *Beijing Literature*, a monthly magazine based in Beijing. He was born in Gong An, Hubei Province, China.

His works have been published in many distinguished Chinese magazines such as *The World Literature*, *Genesis*, *Essays*, *Shanhua*, *Youth Literature*, *Poetry Journal*, etc.

Gili HAIMOVICH is a poet and translator published internationally.

She writes in both English and Hebrew and has volumes of poetry in Hebrew and a selection of poetry originally written in English, *Living on a Blank Page*. This selection has been published in two editions; the second one includes Gili's photographic work. Her sixth volume, *Landing Lights*, appeared early in 2017 in Israel (Iton 77 Publishing House).

Gili's poetry has been published internationally in numerous journals and anthologies, such as *Poetry International*, *International Poetry Review*, *Poem: International English Language Quarterly*, *Asymptote*, *Drain Magazine*, *Literary Review of Canada (LRC)*, *Blue Lyra*, *Circumference*, *Poetry Repairs*, *TOK1 – Writing the New Toronto 1*, *Ezra Magazine*, *Lilith*, *Bridges*, and *Recours au Poème* (Translated into French) as well as main Israeli journals and anthologies such as *The Most Beautiful Poems in Hebrew* (Yedioth Ahronot Books, 2013).

She has translated into Hebrew poets such Fiona Samson, Lois Michel Unger, Micael Dikel and Dara Barnat and into English, leading Israeli poets such as Nurit Zarchi and Yehezkel Nafshi. Her translations have appeared or are forthcoming in journals such as *Poetry International*, *Asymptote*, *Blue Lyra*, *Mediterranean Poetry* and *Poetry Repairs*.

She received a grant nominating her as an outstanding artist by the Israeli Ministry of Immigrant Absorption (2014). Also in 2014, *Baby Girl* won a grant from Acum – the Israeli artists' association, as did her most recent book, *Landing Lights*. Her book, *Reflected Like Joy*, received a grant from the Pais Commity for Arts and Culture. Gili also works as writing-focused intermodal arts therapist and creative writing educator.

Canadian poet **Akin JEJE** lives in Hong Kong and his works have been published and featured in both Canada and Hong Kong.

Jeje's first work, 'Dreaming of The Sands', was published in Canada in 1999. His first full-length poetry collection, *Smoked Pearl: Poems of Hong Kong and Beyond* was a semi-finalist for the 2009 International Proverse Prize, and was published by Proverse Hong Kong in 2010. Jeje's most recent publication is 'Death of Chivalry' in *Quixotica; Poems East of La Mancha* (Chameleon Press, 2016).

Susan LAVENDER is an actress, poet, solicitor, radio newsreader, and a member of Hong Kong Peel Street Poets and Liars' League HK.

She studied acting and theatre arts in London in the seventies and continues to perform in theatre, films, videos, poetry and story-telling events, often writing her own material.

Anglo-Italian by birth, she is bilingual in English and Italian and is a registered official translator at the Italian Consulate in Hong Kong.

Liv LUNDBERG (b. 1944) is Professor emerita in Creative Writing, University of Tromsø, 1993 - 2014. Her first of nine books of poetry, *The clear tone*, was published in 1979 and her most recent, *When I do not belong*, in 2008. Other publications include two novels and a selection of essays. A selection of her poetry appeared in 2012. Single poems have been translated into several languages.

She has translated into Norwegian five books of poetry, the most recent (2010) being by Shuntaro Tanikawa.

Liv Lundberg has participated in international poetry festivals in Scandinavia, Struga, Malaysia, South Africa, Medellin, Colombia, the Shaar festival in Israel, Estonia, Lithuania, and Romania.

Marta MARKOSKA (1981, Skopje) graduated from the Department of Comparative Literature at the Faculty of Philology "Blaze Koneski" in Skopje, and earned her master's degree in Interdisciplinary Cultural Studies in Literature at the Institute of Macedonian Literature in Skopje.

She is the first recipient of the Todor Chalovski Prize awarded to a young Macedonian writer to recognize exceptional promise and contribution in the fields of poetry, literary criticism, essays and creative writing. The award resulted in publication of the bi-lingual (Macedonian-English) edition of the book *Black Holes Within Us* by GALIKUL (Association for culture, literature and art from Skopje), founded in 2007 by Todor Chalovski (1945-2015), one of the most eminent Macedonian writers.

Markoska has eight publications to date. Besides the above-mentioned book, she is also author of *Black Holes Within Us* (poetry, first edition), Skopje, Macedonia, House of Culture "Koco Racin", 2014; *Culture and Memory* (cultural studies), Skopje, Macedonia, "Matica Makedonska", 2014; *Discussion on Zen Buddhism: Religious and Philosophical Transcendence Between Eastern and Western Thought* (scientific study), Skopje, Macedonia, "Matica Makedonska", 2013; *Headfirst Towards The Heights* (poetry, second edition), Skopje, Macedonia, "Magor", 2013; *Headfirst Toward The Heights* (poetry, first edition), Radovish, Macedonia, OU Centre for Culture "Aco Karamanov", 2012; *Hyper Hypotheses* (essays), Skopje, Macedonia, Institute of Macedonian Literature, 2011; *Whirlpool in Bethlehem* (stories), Skopje, Macedonia, Templum, 2010; and *All Tributaries Flow Into My Basin* (poetry), Skopje, Macedonia, Templum, 2009.

Markoska is a recipient of the following awards: "Aco Karamanov" (2012), for the poetic manuscript "Headfirst Toward The Heights" and "Beli Mugri" (2014), for the poetry manuscript "Black Holes Within Us." Also, she won an award in the "Nova Makedonija" 2015 short story competition for, 'Heights of Felix' and was a first place winner of the 2007 "Elektrolit" 2007 short story competition for, 'What happens when you're reading Frazer'. Her work is included in several anthologies of contemporary poetry and prose.

She has been a member of the Writers' Association of Macedonia since 2012.

MATHURA, (Margus LATTIK), is an Estonian writer and translator, author of eight collections of poetry.

He received the Gustav Suits Poetry Award (2014) and the Regional Award of the Cultural Endowment of Estonia (2004). He won the International Bhakti Writers Contest (2013).

Keith NUNES is from Lake Rotoma, New Zealand.

He was a newspaper sub-editor for 20-plus years but after a nervous breakdown he changed lanes and now writes from a different perspective.

He has been published around the globe and is a Pushcart Prize nominee. His chapbook, *Crashing the Calliope*, is available for sale.

Sam POWNEY is a writer and professional editor with a background in Chinese language.

He has been based for several years in Hong Kong, where he is a recent and enthusiastic participant in the emerging poetry scene at Peel Street Poetry and Poetry OutLoud.

Leading a peripatetic existence for most of his childhood and adult life, he has spent time in Greece, Albania, the US, India, China, France, Germany, and occasionally in Britain, where he was born. He does not like to be thought of as a Shropshire lad. Nevertheless, he admits enjoying Housman in spite of himself, saying, "Housman didn't live in Shropshire, so I like to think we have that in common."

He is fascinated by a great range of poetry, but particularly responds to the natural images and metaphors of familiar landscapes, especially that of Greece, southern India, and parts of China. For this reason, his greats are Sappho, translations from the Tamil poets by AK Ramanujan, and many of the Tang and Song dynasty masters, to whom he was first introduced while studying Chinese at Edinburgh University. That being said, he also takes a great deal from Basho and the crisp West Coast imagery of Gary Snyder.

Sam's poems explore a variety of forms, from the penta/heptasyllabic styles of East Asia, to comedy tetrameter à la Hilaire Belloc. Still open to new influences, he immensely enjoys the experience of sharing with other poets, considering himself, "extremely fortunate to have stumbled into a vibrant community of poets in the midst of Hong Kong's outwardly anodyne environment."

Vaughan RAPATAHANA is a Hong Kong permanent resident, with homes also in the Philippines and Aotearoa New Zealand.

He is published widely across several genres, in his two main languages, Maori and English.

His latest poetry collection, *Atonement*, has been nominated for a National Book Award in the Philippines and his instigated and co-edited language critique, *Why English? Confronting the Hydra* was published in the UK by Multilingual Matters, UK, in June 2016.

Angelo RIZZI
(b. Italy, 1956) is a multilingual poet, having written poems in Arabic, Spanish, and Italian.

He took part in the UNESCO 2006 conference on the theme, "Dialogue among Nations". He has won many literary awards and has participated in poetry meetings in Rome, Havana, Paris and Curtea de Argeş.

Glória SOFIA (Gloria Sofia Varela MONTEIRO) (b. Cape Verde, 14 February 1985) is a poet and publisher.

She graduated in engineering and nature conservation management in the University of the Azores and has worked as an assistant in the Ecology Department at the University.

In 2014, together with Osvaldo Brito, she founded EDITORA BRIAL.

Her own published work includes the following book-titles: *Poesia das Lágrimas* (Poetry of tears), Chiado Editora, Lisbon, Portugal, 2013; and *Laços de Poesia* (Ties of poetry), Editora Brial, Rotterdam, Holland, 2014.

The latter has been translated as follows: *Rubans De Poésies* (Ties of poetry), traduit par Rocha Marie, Editora Brial, Rotterdam, Holland, 2014; *Intrecci Di Poesia* (Ties of poetry), Traduzione di Dulcineida Gomes, Editora Brial, Rotterdam, Holland, 2016.

Along with work by others, her work has appeared in the following anthologies: *Horizonte da Poesia VI* (Horizon Poetry VI), Euedito, Portugal, 2014; and *Palavras da Alma* (Soul words), Editora Brial, Rotterdam, Holland, 2015.

In 2015, Glória was nominated as a candidate for the Rolex Mentor and Protégé Arts Initiative. In 2016, she participated in the literary festival, "International Festival Curtea de Argeş Poetry Nights" in Romania.

Hayley SOLOMON is a New Zealand author, librarian and poet. She holds a Master of Arts Degree through the University of Victoria, Wellington, and has eighteen published historical romance fiction titles to her credit.

She is a three time Honoree of the University of Maine at Machias, has twice been selected for the annual Momaya Press International short story anthology, was a regency romance 'top pick' by *Romantic Times* for her novel *Raven's Ransom*, and is currently writing her second Jane Austen *Pride and Prejudice* variation.

Dr Dong SUN (b. 1969) is a poet and professor of foreign languages at Nanjing University of Finance and Economics.

Originally from the northeast of China, she studied at the Qiqihar Normal University, Heilongjiang University, and Nanjing University. In 2003 she was a visiting researcher at the University of Waterloo, Ontario, Canada. She did her post-doctoral studies at McMaster University in Hamilton, Canada from 2009-2010.

Her first collection of poetry *Cruel Crow*, co-authored with Feng Dong, was published in 2011. She has published nearly a hundred poems in various literary journals and online media in Chinese, English, French and Romanian. Currently Dr. Sun works at the State University of New York.

Luisa TERNAU was born in Trieste, Italy.

Since her childhood she has always loved literature.

The love of knowledge and a wish to explore the world have taken Luisa to live in London and in Cardiff (UK), in Japan, the USA and in Hong Kong.

Her inspiration is found in the people and landscapes she has encountered and in her extensive reading of literature from several parts of the world, including epic poems and fairy tales.

Mavisel YENER was born in 1962 in Ankara and graduated from the Dentistry Faculty of Ege University in 1984. She is one of the most renowned contemporary Turkish authors and has written over 100 children's, young adult and adult books. She has devoted her life to children's literature. She has written in many genres, including children's novels, poems, short stories, fairy tales, radio plays and theatre scripts. Her short stories, fairy tales and poems are also included in textbooks for schools.

She has worked as an editor of many children's and young adult books. She prepared and presented two radio programmes, "Sounds in our Hearts" and "Book Worm". She writes book reviews and articles in the literature supplement of the newspaper, *Cumhuriyet*.

Yener gives workshops on children's literature, and attends symposiums on children's literature all around the world; she also gives lectures at universities. She represented Turkey at Tiran and Split at "Literature in Flux", an annual organization aiming to connect literary centres of Europe, in 2012.

She won her first award when she was just sixteen. In later years, as her work thrived, she won many acclaimed awards and recognitions including, in 2002, First Prize in both the Samim Kocagöz Short Story Award, and the Ömer Seyfettin Short Story Award. She won the ÇGYD Awards Best Children's Poetry Award (2004), ÇGYD Awards Last 15 Years Best Children's Poetry Book Special Prize (2009), and Kosovo 2013's Best Children's Author Award. Most recently she has been honored by being nominated for the 2018 Hans Christian Andersen Award.

Her literary works have been translated into a number of languages. She is a member of P.E.N. Various papers, MA and PhD theses have been written about her work. Her books have also been produced in braille.

Carter VANCE is a student and aspiring poet originally from Cobourg, Ontario, currently studying at Carleton University in Ottawa. His work has appeared in such publications as *The Vehicle*, *(parenthetical)* and *F(r)iction*, and also appears on his blog, "Comment is Welcome". He received an Honourable Mention from Contemporary Verse 2's Young Buck Poetry Awards in 2015.

EDITORS' BRIEF BIOGRAPHIES

Gillian BICKLEY, born and educated in the United Kingdom, has lived mostly in Hong Kong since 1970.

Her poetry collections include *For the Record and other Poems of Hong Kong, Moving House and other Poems from Hong Kong, Sightings, China Suite, Perceptions* and the bilingual English-Romanian *Poems.* Two collections – *Moving House* and *For the Record* – have also been published in Chinese; individual poems have been published in Arabic, Catalan, Chinese, Czech, French, German, Romanian, Turkish and other languages. In 2014, she was awarded the "Grand Prix Orient-Occident Des Arts" at the 18th International Festival, "Curtea de Argeş Poetry Nights", held in Romania. Gillian Bickley is one of the Hong Kong poets discussed in Agnes S. L. Lam's study, *Becoming poets: The Asian English Experience.*

Gillian has written or edited several non-fiction books in different fields: *The Golden Needle: The Biography of Frederick Stewart, 1836-1889 (founder of Hong Kong Government Education)*, Hong Kong Baptist University and David C. Lam Institute for East-West Studies, 1997; *Hong Kong Invaded! A '97 Nightmare*, University of Hong Kong Press, Hong Kong, 2001; *The Development of Education in Hong Kong, 1841-1897: as revealed through the Early Education Reports of the Hong Kong Government, 1848-1896*, Proverse Hong Kong, Hong Kong, 2002; *The Stewarts of Bourtreebush*, Centre for Scottish Studies, University of Aberdeen, Scotland, 2003; *A Magistrate's*

Court in 19ᵗʰ Century Hong Kong: Court in Time, Proverse Hong Kong, first edition, 2005; second edition, 2009; *The Complete Court Cases of Magistrate Frederick Stewart*, Proverse Hong Kong, 2008; *In Time of War* (in collaboration with Richard Collingwood-Selby), an edition based on the writings of Henry C.S. Collingwood-Selby (1898-1992), Lieutenant Commander in the Royal Navy, Proverse Hong Kong, 2013.

Five of these twelve English-language books received publication support from Hong Kong Arts Development Council (HKADC) and three from Lord Wilson Heritage Trust. The extensive research necessary for six of the non-fiction works listed was made possible by research grants awarded by the Hong Kong Baptist University.

Dr Bickley was Senior Lecturer / Associate Professor in the Department of English at the Hong Kong Baptist University for twenty-two years. She has been a full-time faculty member at the University of Lagos, Nigeria; the University of Auckland, New Zealand; and at the University of Hong Kong.

For several years, Gillian was an adjudicator at the world-famous Hong Kong Schools Music & Speech Association's annual Speech Festival and has also been a judge for the Budding Poets' Society Hong Kong.

More recently, as co-ordinator of literary activities for the English-Speaking Union Hong Kong, a non-profit registered educational charity, she has led reading appreciation sessions which are open to the community and assists to deliver reading courses at local schools. She has worked with the Gifted Education Section of the Education Bureau to encourage creative writing among students. On a freelance basis, she has completed teaching creative reading / writing courses at the Hong Kong Academy for Gifted Education (HKAGE) and at the University of Hong Kong School for Professional and Continuing Education (HKU SPACE) and been a guest lecturer on poetry at Lingnan University Community College. Her creative reading /

writing course at HKU SPACE continues to be offered. In 2016, she managed twenty and hosted seventeen meet-the-author events at a Hong Kong bookshop.

Following her career in academia, Gillian has become an experienced project-manager, text editor, and production manager, including of poetry, non-fiction, fiction and academic writing.

She has been a member of the Society of Authors in the United Kingdom since her school days.

Verner BICKLEY was born in the North-West of England, and educated there, in Wales and London, and has lived in Asian and Pacific countries for over fifty years. He has been scholar, teacher, manager, broadcaster, stage and film actor and cultural diplomat in a life often enlivened by music and song, dance and entertainment.

Verner's many scholarly articles and book publications are mainly on educational and cross-cultural topics. He has however also published two volumes of memoirs: *Footfalls Echo in the Memory* and *Steps To Paradise And Beyond*. His five-book graded poetry anthology, *Poems to Enjoy*, has been popular since the 1960s. These now benefit from accompanying recordings of all poems in the texts (read mostly by himself, but some by his wife Gillian), as well as from teaching and performance notes. He is a member of the United Kingdom Society of Authors.

With his wife, Gillian, Verner Bickley is joint-publisher of Proverse Hong Kong and co-founder of the Proverse Prize and the Proverse Poetry Prize.

Verner was a naval officer in pre-independent Sri Lanka and India. He served in the Colonial Education Service in Singapore and, later, as a British Council officer in post-independence Burma, Indonesia and Japan. In Hawaii from 1971 to 1981, he served as the Director of the Culture Learning Institute at the East-West Center, established by the US Congress in Hawaii in 1960 and functioning as a US-based institution for public diplomacy with international governance, staffing, students and Fellows.

From 1972 to 1980, Verner led a small team of anthropologists, cross-cultural psychologists and linguists, focusing on the different ways in which individuals and whole societies cope in bicultural and multicultural contexts and how they address problems presented by different cultural norms. Among many interesting projects, his Institute provided for the pioneering voyage of the canoe, *Hōkūle'a*, from Hawaii to Tahiti, disproving the theories of Thor Heyerdahl.

Verner was instrumental in bringing to conferences in Honolulu writers who included Guy Amirthanayagam, Leon Edel, Vincent Eri, Nissim Ezekial, Reuel Denney, Janet Frame, Allen Ginsberg, Syd Harrex, Thomas Keneally, Maxine Hong-Kingston, Arun Kolatkhar, Ananda Murthy, Kenzaburo Oe, Kushwant Singh, Kamala Markandaya, RK Narayan, AK Ramanajuan, ER Sarachchandra, Wole Soyinka and Albert Wendt.

After leaving Hawaii, and while in Saudia Arabia for a two-year assignment with the national airline, Saudia, Verner was responsible for a multi-national staff of 100 persons, mainly, but not exclusively, in Jeddah and Riyadh.

In 1893, Verner was appointed founding director of the Institute of Language in Education in Hong Kong and held that post until 1992.

Refusing to retire, Verner continues to live in Hong Kong where he writes and publishes on a variety of topics and devotes himself to the English-Speaking Union (Hong Kong) as Chairman of its Executive Committee. In that capacity he travels every year to the Mainland of China to join other judges of the national Public-Speaking Competition organised by national media. He has been an adjudicator for the Hong Kong Schools Music and Speech Association's annual Speech Festival for many years and for a while was Representative in Hong Kong for Trinity College London.

Verner Bickley's experiences have created in him an interest in cross-cultural experiences and attitudes and in a desire to communicate what he has learnt. Through his memoirs as well as his personal contacts, he hopes not only to interest others, but to encourage them to build on their own desire to learn about and empathise with other cultures.

PROVERSE HONG KONG

Together, Gillian and Verner Bickley are the publishers of Proverse Hong Kong, a Hong Kong-based press which publishes both local and international authors, including non-native speakers of English. They are also co-founders of two annual international literary prizes for work submitted in English: in 2008, they founded the Proverse Prize for unpublished book-length fiction, non-fiction or poetry, and, in 2016, they established the Proverse Poetry Prize (for single poems which may have been previously published in a language other than English). In the case of both prizes, entries are received from around the world.

Beginning in 2007 up to October 2016, Proverse has managed, edited and published about 90 English-language books by Hong Kong and international writers, five Chinese-language books and one English / Chinese bilingual book. Of the English-language books, about seventeen have been awarded publication support by Hong Kong Arts Development Council (HKADC) and one by Lord Wilson Heritage Trust. One received a publication grant from the Ministry of Culture of the Czech Republic and one received a publication grant from the Ministry of Culture and Tourism of the Republic of Turkey.

Twice a year, Proverse organises literary events in Hong Kong, open to the public. New books are launched, writers are introduced and launching authors give brief talks. Announcements are made relating to the current year's Proverse Prize and Proverse Poetry Prize and prizes are presented to those authors who are present.

Gillian and Verner work hard to bring authors before the reading public. In 2016, they arranged twenty meet-the-author sessions, held at a Hong Kong bookshop. Edited videos of these talks are available on Youtube.

Of the titles published by Proverse, several have attracted a Preface or advance appreciation from figures of international reputation, most notably perhaps, from Václav

Havel (for the English translation of Olga Walló's *Tightrope: A Bohemian Tale*).

Two titles (Peter Gregoire's, *Article 109* and *The Devil You Know*) were best sellers at Dymocks Hong Kong.

The publication by Proverse of the late Sophronia Liu's book, *A Shimmering Sea*, was a major argument in the award to Sophronia of a posthumous PhD at the University of Minnesota.

Other writers published by Proverse have also benefited in their literary careers.

Gillian's and Verner's books and all those by other authors, published by Proverse, are available internationally as well as locally, including through the Chinese University of Hong Kong Press, and there are copies in the British Library and other legal deposit libraries in the United Kingdom.

NOTES AND COMMENTARIES

[1] Luisa Ternau comments on her poem, 'A Metropolitan Vision' as follows:
"This poem questions the competitive attitude that is predominant in contemporary society. Skyscrapers aim to reach the clouds (which hover high in the sky and yet what do clouds stand for? Clouds are unclear in shape and hide a meaning that people are striving to find). Meanwhile on a more "earthly" level students try their best to win prizes in sports and other school activities. All this competitiveness is fueled by dreams to be the best. The poem suggests that maybe only upon death (when our own sun moves beyond the horizon) the true meaning of all this competitiveness will be disclosed. Therefore the attributes of dreams are the most varied: thin, solid, large and candid. The comparison of the dreams' candour to cheerful clouds gives a positive note to the finale. The poem aims to suggest that life is bright in its multiple colours, sounds and shapes and yet at the core of it stays something vague as a dream, which is not necessarily a nightmare."

[2] Maria Elena Blanco writes about her poem, 'Abandoned to their Pleasure, Khajuraho', as follows:
"The setting is an erotic sculpture, carved in one of the sandstone walls of the Parsvanatha Temple at Khajuraho, India, which shows a woman in the position of removing a thorn from her foot, curiously not stooping, but rather raising her bent leg to her torso with a graceful sway of her body. This inspires the reflection on a woman's attitude towards her own body and her physical and mental relationship with her environment, both outwardly and inwardly. In turn, an association is made with another image which has deeply impressed the poet: the 15th century tapestries seen at the Musée de Cluny in Paris: *La Dame à la licorne*, or The Lady of the Unicorn, where a

woman is also shown in the midst of the natural world, the animals and objects that surround her daily life, and whose enigmatic stance in that environment leads the poet to reflect on desire and its relation to life and death."

[3] Maria Elena Blanco comments on 'All-Purpose River, Varanasi', as follows:
"Another poem inspired by India: the background for this poem is a boat-ride on the Ganges at sunrise at a point where one approaches the open pyre where the dead are cremated according to ancient religious rites. This image gives rise to reflections on the contrasts perceived in that very sacred city of Varanasi, formerly also known as Benares, between the sheer vividness and proliferation of colours, shapes, textures, simultaneous social and religious sceneries, and the potent spirituality of the local religious traditions, bent on a cult of the void expressed in the most material of forms."

[4] Liv Lundberg says this about her poem, 'Atlantic':
"I wrote this poem on the occasion of the opening of the International PEN World Congress in Tromsø, Norway, 2004.
    Tromsø is the biggest city (a mini-metropolis) in the north of Norway, far above the Arctic Circle, where I was born and raised and where I have been living most of my life. I also lived seven years even farther north and east, at the island of the North Cape and in Pasvik Valley close to the Russian border, in the seventies when the Russian border was closed.
    In 1995-96 I travelled for three months in several African countries, and ended up in Cape Town, which I have visited three more times since then. In 1998, I published a book of poems titled 'africa.'

The Atlantic Ocean is for me the closest connection between North and South.

Living at the end of the world, you have a privileged perspective on the world, different from the central mega-cities."

[5] Marta Markoska writes this about her poem, '(Else)Where?':
"Buddhists say peace comes from within and that, if it is truly reached, nothing in the world can disturb us very much.

Humanity must find a way to understand that everyone here is on the right path, even at those times when we feel completely lost. So, however illogical our situation may seem at the moment, finding our true soulfulness – which, at the same time, paradoxically, is actually selflessness – we will immediately understand the way towards ourselves. Every single one of us lives on the Earth on 'lease'; but we act as if life itself starts with us, 'and with us it shall end' (a line from my poem 'Quantum Theory of Love', in *Black Holes Within Us*, 2016, p. 99).

A man can only live in his present moment and in acceptance of it, however that moment seems impossible to accept. Because, even tomorrow when we wake up, it will be today! If the poem sounds a little bit melancholic, that is because of our subconscious feeling that everything is transcendent.

Happiness starts within us. Not with our money, job, status, relationships. The moral of the poem is: find peace with yourself and accept your hard times and the dark places you've been, because, however paradoxical it sounds, actually, finding our way in, gives us the way out."

[6] Keith Nunes has given the following introduction to his poem, 'Escape From Absolution':

"This poem originated from my previous home in a rural community called Oropi, 25km south of Tauranga in the New Zealand province of the Bay of Plenty in the North Island. Behind our house, through the back gate, were 1200 hectares of protected virgin native forest. The house was 300 metres above sea level and cold in the winter but crisp and clear in the spring/autumn evenings – you could see stars forever.

The original New Zealanders were Maori from the Polynesian islands (1000 years ago) and their warrior culture meant the British were pressed hard when trying to conquer the country during the 1800s. Hence the reference to warriors and armies in the poem.

The native birds are as fascinating as the history of the region and the density and haunting air of the forest led me to create the poem.

I feel the kiwi bird is a symbol of my home and is 'tattooed' on the inside of my eyelids branding me a Kiwi! The kiwi bird, as well as all other native birds, are constantly fighting for survival against introduced species – and by the same token so too are the indigenous Maori who have suffered at the hands of colonisation and in some sense been battered and are striving for a revolution (change).

We as a nation need to focus on the people who are struggling ('save me')."

[7] Akin Jeje says that his poem, 'Hues of the Storm', is simply described:
"[It is] a contrast between the beauty of a thunderstorm observed in the heart of Kowloon [in Hong Kong SAR] with the pervading pollution that threatens to overwhelm the purity of the storm with the dullness of the smog after. I was inspired by a storm I experienced in Mong Kok years ago."

[8] Of 'Intertexting in India', Maria Elena Blanco writes:
"This poem is the result of the drawn-out process of writing a requested text for an anthology in homage of a well-known Spanish poet, Miguel Hernández. It traces the difficult task of writing a *poème de circonstance*, for which the poet must first find a motivation, a link to her own experience, in order to be able to connect poetically with the subject matter, in spite of having been familiar with many aspects of that subject matter previously, as part of her literary education. Without a deep personal connection no poetry seems to be possible, but when that connection is found a sort of alchemy happens and both the subject matter and the poet's consciousness are understood in a new light. That connection was unexpectedly found in India, spurred by the reading of another poet's work."

[9] Mathura explains some points about his poem, 'Light Of Bones':
"The poem takes its opening line and inspiration from the work of a contemporary Swedish poet Pär Hansson who wrote his first book while residing in an old dilapidated house in the north of Sweden. For many years, our family had a similar house in the woods of Estonia where I loved to go writing. Its ramshackle state had a special creative appeal for me. Somehow, the place was very authentic and real."

In response to a question, Mathura explained that the word "welfare" is used in the poem as a critique of the welfare society which oftentimes sets material welfare as an end in itself.

[10] Dong SUN has given the following notes on the text of her poem, 'My Typical Day':

"The world is yours": second stanza, line 1:
"Chairman Mao made this remark in his 17 May 1957 address to young Chinese students studying in Moscow University. Translated into English, his original words are, 'The world is yours and is ours as well, but it will be yours in the end.' Here I allude to the remarks ironically. The young living in today's world, destroyed by their fathers (in an environmental sense), are no longer the masters of the future."

"flowerpox in the flower basket": first stanza, line 5:
"Smallpox is "天花" in Chinese, meaning heavenly flowers. I use "flowerpox" here in order to make sense in English without losing its Chinese connotations."

"Old Beetles": second stanza, line 3:
"Beetles have several meanings: firstly, they feed on rotten things. Also, in Egyptian culture, they are considered holy. Again, in ancient China, there was a tradition of putting beetles in the mouths of the dead for fear they might, at their judgement after death, say something unfavorable to their afterlife."

"Bitter ocean and rosy lips" third stanza, line 2:
"'Bitter ocean and rosy lips' are metaphors in Chinese, referring to hardships and love in secular life."

[11] Hei Feng wrote this about his poem, 'Night Is Still Firing Guns':
"I always think that human beings need to live in symbiosis with the world. We interact with our surroundings and with other creatures in an ever-changing and transformative process. The strong should not eat the weak. It is important for us to respect other living beings and also material things. This respect derives from a humanistic view but is

also religious. It should be our original and ultimate goal. I have loathed killing since I was little. The background of my poem is the experience of witnessing a killing at night, back in my home village. There I also learnt and witnessed the abuse of fertilizers, the pollution of rivers and the death from cancer of my childhood playmates. I wrote this poem in astonishment. The world is becoming depraved, with no conscience; there are few good things left for us. I only wish that my poems can live for those killed animals and that my pen, flying in the jungle of words, can give them rebirth."

In response to a question, Hei Feng replied, "'Sack' here refers to nylon bags of animal meat".

[12] Hayley Solomon has given this comment about her poem, 'Once Grown, Now Gone, and Green No More… Ode To The Environment And Our Planet':

"This poem is a philosophical reflection on today's careless consumer age. We've become creatures of instant gratification, spoilt and inconsiderate. Our planet's significant signs of wear are intimations of our own destruction. Self-responsibility must be preeminent if we are to move forward positively.

I was moved to write this after reflecting that pollutants from fossil fuels make it literally impossible to breathe in certain highly populated, energy intensive cities; that the consumption of aerosols, petrol, diesel, coal and other emissions from a post industrial world are a causative effect of global warming, that polar ice caps are melting, that ice sheets are causing massive implications for marine life, sea levels and thus land subsidence and retention. Further, deforestation of our planet is happening both by this phenomenon, and through our general carelessness in terms of felling, logging and poor conservation policies. I acknowledge that the slow, gradual impact on our planet might be the work of millennia, but time is not a mitigating factor for nonchalance or negligence.

I hope, through the process of thinking, reading, learning and being sensitized to issues, we can all, collectively, as humans on this earth, make a small difference and positive imprint on our beautiful planet."

[13] Gili Haimovich wrote this about her poem, Pedestrians' Cheer':

"I happen to be a pedestrian. Not because I made a deliberate choice; I just lack a driver's license. I took a few driving lessons not long ago. Until then, I had not been aware that being a pedestrian points to something in my character. Yet after the initial joy of finding myself behind the wheel I realized that walking was, among other things, a statement of my own independence.

Being a pedestrian entails a contradiction. I can describe it as having a skin too thin. On the physical level, walking exposes me to weather too harsh on my fair skin. But on an internal – perhaps metaphorical – level, walking lets me experience my surroundings more directly.

Walking is a humbling experience and yet, it can offer an immediate, albeit tiny, sense of freedom. As a pedestrian, the journey from one point to another allows you to explore – in personal and almost secretive ways – your surroundings and yourself in relation to them no matter who you are: a woman who has a pass made at her in the street, a weary parent with a querulous child in tow, or a person who roams the conflicted political reality of Israel.

Above all, there is value in choices that we make not in pursuit of comfort but in the pursuit of alternatives to categorical, non-personal, and mainstream choices. There is value in finding ways to take part in a landscape without taking it over."

[14] Luisa Ternau explains her poem, 'Plastic Soul Recycling' as follows:
"This poem questions the existence of a soul in artificial, man-made objects. Such soul does seem to exist as something that is attributed to the objects by the people who handle them (like plastic flowers and dolls). Natural elements are perceived in a different way than the objects which are made artificially to resemble them. Thus natural flowers are opposed to plastic ones. The poem suggests that artificial, man-made objects might as well have a soul. What happens to this soul when its corresponding objects get recycled? In nature, natural things, once dead, recycle slowly while their souls wander in a different dimension. The poem suggests that in the same way the souls of artificial objects, which were loved or despised by the people who happened at some point to deal with them, upon reaching recycling stage, follow the same course of transforming into a new status. The natural world and the artificial, man-made world are counterposed but at the same time both worlds interact to give an image of complex and dynamic reality."

[15] Commenting on her poem, 'Psalm', Joy Al-Sofi wrote:
"I have a longtime concern for the environment and am passionately opposed to the destruction of the biosphere of our beautiful planet by the powers that be. More and more devastation in the past few years, including the blowout of an ocean oil rig in the Gulf of Mexico that continued to spew oil for 87 days in 2010, the melting of the ice caps and permafrost which has released the trapped stores of methane and virulent, bio-hazardous bacteria and viruses, have led me to think about the many people who, with good

intentions, turn to their holy texts only to find them silent on this issue, which in turn encourages them to embrace denial.

I wish to advocate for the Earth by using words; words of and from the King James version of the Bible and particularly the Book of Psalms. Those who are familiar with this translation will not fail to recognize the references and, perhaps, they will be moved to help us save our world, ourselves."

[16] Glória Sofia Varela Monteiro comments on her poem, 'Rain', as follows:
"In my land, in my life and in my world, there is lightning, there are people and times that break my heart. In the midst of these whirlwinds of feelings there sometimes comes a liquid light that, in the poem, I name as rain. It extinguishes the rage and makes life flourish in my soul."

[17] Maria Elena Blanco explains that her poem, 'Reversible Fields', was written during a poetry workshop with the American poet Anne Waldman at the *Schule für Dichtung in Wien* (Vienna School for Poetry), in which one of the challenges proposed was to write about parts, or partitions. "This poem, conceptually as well as visually, is made up of two parts, which evolve from a movement towards greater complexity and completeness and then to a gradual detachment from possessions and self. As in, 'Abandoned To Their Pleasure, Khajuraho' [*q.v., Mingled Voices... 2016*, pp. 18-19], the subject is a woman, and the *chiaroscuro* treatment reflects the evolution from light to dark, which – curiously – is a movement from weightiness to lightness. In the end, fulfillment is only found in the total, dual, image, whose parts or partitions are inseparable from each other."

[18] This is how Carter Vance describes his poem, 'Smoker's Cough':

"This poem was intended to reflect the duality of what we are as people when meeting someone for the first time. At once, we try to be open, clear, presenting a picture of ourselves that is authentic and clear, much like the cellophane wrapping on the cigarette carton. A certain cliché might describe this exercise as the presentation of our "best self" to the world, and in particular those we wish to have some sort of greater connection with. At the same time, we are guarded, pulling back on certain aspects of our selves that we imagine as off-putting or beyond the conventional. It is this contradiction that drives the human attempt to understand and connect with each other, as we parcel out those details in ways we think likely to further the connection without severing it.

This poem may have a particular setting, namely the train stations of central London, ever-ringed by outside smokers and last night's litter, but its essential point travels no matter where we find ourselves. As long as we seek new friends, and maybe something more, in new places, these feelings echo."

In reponse to a question, Carter Vance explained, "'Brown PoMo' refers to shades of brown which were prominently used in post-modern design, mainly in the 1970s."

[19] Of her poem, 'Special Objects', Maria Elena Blanco writes:

"This poem was also [*see note 17 above*] written at the Anne Waldman workshop as an exercise to integrate various elements coming from totally different sources of inspiration and personal experiences – those of others – combined with one's own. Again, in order to succeed poetically, one must personalize those foreign elements and relate them to one's experience or sphere of associations, thus transforming them into something different from their prior essence in a sort of alchemical process which appropriates, divests and recreates them into new life."

[20] Luisa Ternau says this about her poem, 'Spring in My Heart':
"This is a poem about the contrast between façade and the truth it hides. Spring is imposed on oneself, therefore it is everywhere! This artificial feeling of blooming and happiness is compared to the artificial snow which makes tourists satisfied during the skiing season. Artificial snow can create a feeling of happiness the same way artificial spring imposed on oneself can lead to one's own happiness, if one is ready to believe in it. An ironic note is given by the fact that indeed spring will come in due course – it is unavoidable – although it may come at a time when it will remain unnoticed, perhaps even to one's own self."

[21] Commenting on his poem 'Sunny Spratly Parasols', Sam Powney says:
"The summer of 2016 was Hong Kong's hottest in fifty years. Sweltering temperatures brought on a sudden lightning storm on the evening of 9 July, thrilling onlookers but also knocking out the power in several tall buildings on Hong Kong island. Even on ordinary days, the city's looming mountains certainly didn't give the impression of 'hills rejoicing' (Psalm 65:12, 98.8), especially when they harboured the kind of clouds described in line 10.

Over the same season there was a steady crescendo of news reports about tensions in the South China Sea due to conflicting territorial claims. Several years ago, I was refreshed to hear a rarely-heard viewpoint on this kind of irredentism from Taiwanese writer and cultural icon Lung Ying-Tai, who said, 'I'm allergic to nationalism. So, what about leaving the islands to the birds and fish?' In fact, the naïve imagination of nationalism frequently conscripts flora and fauna as well as natural features into its cartographic simulacra. I believe many poets share the sense that nature, while dramatic and beautiful, is not our friend, and that man's claims over it ring hollow.

The form came about largely in response to a poem of Du Fu in the 'ballad' style, which is characterised by heptasyllabic lines interspersed with pentasyllabic questions. Needless to say, 'Ballad of Beauties' (「麗人行」) is a world away from this poem, but I was intrigued to see Du Fu using ostensibly fatuous inquiries to get to the heart of his era's key political issues, hence my own infantile questions taken from familiar children's jokes/songs/Sunday school hymns.

On the ending, the North Pacific ocean to the east of the South China Sea, now home to the 'Pacific trash vortex', is also the breeding ground for the region's powerful typhoons."

[22] Maria Elena Blanco writes about, 'Temple of Chamundi, Mysore':
"Another poem in a series of Indian poems. This poem tells of a visit to a temple where the goddess was not to be seen, as her inner chamber was closed to the public, but the poet was able to observe some of the comings and goings of those who prepare and adorn the temples and the actual sculptural representations of the gods and goddesses who are worshipped there. The poet is drawn to the spontaneous and silent aspect of such worship, in which flowers and animals play a major part, as well as, once again, to its ultimate relationship with the void."
teocallis: ancient Nahua temples (Mexico) (here used metaphorically).

[23] Susan Lavender wrote this about her poem, 'The 69 Club':

"Recently I risked dying from a ruptured appendix and I started worrying that my 93-year old mother might seriously outlive me, with no one younger to care for her. So I wrote this poem about two generations, two different life views, two different life spans...

One is the hippie generation, symbolised by the August 1969 music festival held at Woodstock, New York State. The other is the generation prior to theirs.

In the late sixties and early seventies several famous musicians died at age twenty-seven and have been referred to as the '27 Club'. In 2016 we have lost many stars from the world of music and acting, who have died around age sixty-nine. So the number sixty-nine in my title recalls both the hippies' Woodstock and the age at which some of us are now bowing out, thus forming a club of our own, 'The 69 Club'.

The hippie culture emphasised peace and love and opposed the wars of the past as well as the ongoing wars of their own time, notably the Vietnam war. The older generation toughed it out through the depression after World War I and spent their youth fighting in World War II. We hippies led easier young lives than our parents, but it seems we are not as resilient as they continue to be, living on into their nineties and even hundreds."

[24] Angelo Rizzi explains the origin of his poem, 'The Essential', as follows:

"One day I was in the city of Nice with two friends. They began to talk to each other, when the first said: 'This disordered world'... And the second said: 'it's chaotic'...
I picked up the two words, then returning by the train home, I had the idea of making a poem. The sense of the poem is simple, either, that the poet has a function or rather

a mission in this world. Poetry has not only a soothing end."

25 Commenting on his poem, 'the rain', Vaughan Rapatahana says, "The poet reflects that the foul weather is a metaphor for the way that he has to dress himself to prevent getting wet, given that his own sadness (the tears) is drenching him anyway."

26 As for his poem, 'tin yan don', Vaughan Rapatahana writes: "I often encountered the eccentric man with the odd mannerisms nearby my home in Tin Yan, Tin Shui Wai, [Hong Kong], and he struck me as Don Quixote-like in his stoic refusal to do anything but his own rather hidden agenda."

27 Joy Al-Sofi explains how her poem, 'White Water', came to be written:
"This year, during the month of July, and until the camera went down, I was watching the live webcam from Brooks Falls, Alaska:
"http://explore.org/live-cams/player/brown-bear-salmon-cam-brooks-falls". (Camera is back up now.)
What's there are bears and the sockeye salmon summer run. The bears are fascinating in their variations of colour, size, fishing techniques and preferred locations. Pacific salmon are overwhelming in their tragic struggles to power upstream to the place where they were born in order to reproduce and die. These sights were immensely moving and led to my writing this new poem, 'White Water'. This is the place beneath the falls where only the biggest bears can stand and not be swept away. The salmon gather here in large numbers to make their leaps. It is a place of the most danger and the greatest opportunities. In the white water is where we are now as a species.

It was impossible to watch this without thinking about the recurring and intersecting cycles of these two species' lives. The ideas extended to the river and what we, humans, are doing to the intricate cycles of life and to ourselves. The last line is an exhortation to humanity to 'wake up.'"

[28] Maria Elena Blanco wrote this about her poem, 'Winter Garden':
"A visit to a friend's house, which in a fleeting moment – a moment that would not have happened had it not been for the fact of forgetting a key and having to go into a certain side room to look for it, a sort of afterthought or coda, coupled with the unexpected sound of a train and a play of shadows on a window – somehow spurs a succession of sensations and memories, awakens a rush of associations, creating a magical instant in the mind of the poet, reminiscent of that provoked in Proust by the taste of the madeleine dipped in his tea. Life copies art and art is a self-generating process. That is what modern literary theory calls inter-textuality, a process that nourishes all the poems submitted [see *Mingled Voices*, pp. 18-19, 20, 27-28, 40, 42, 45, 54-55]."

[29] Aytül Akal gives this explanation of the subject and inspiration for her children's poem, 'A Boat on the House', which was originally published in Turkish in the book, *Denizin Büyüsü*:
"Some decades ago, during a summer vacation, I was in, Kaş, Antalya Province (Turkey) and made a day trip to Kekova Island, an area rich in Lycian, Byzantine and Roman ruins. The ruins are under the sea and we saw the walls of ancient houses from the boat. (It was not allowed to dive there.) I wondered then, if people living in those houses ever imagined that hundreds or thousands of years later, a boat would sail over their houses. I was particularly

interested in the fate of the Lycian city of Simena, which is thought to have sunk into the sea after an earthquake during the second century AD. (By the way, the name "Kekova", is "Dolichiste" in the Lycian language.)

A few years ago the government decided to build a dam (Yortanli Dam) on the ruins of Allianoi, near Bergama, İzmir (Smyrna), where many civilizations had lived from the prehistoric era onwards. There were many protests, but all was in vain. As soon as the dam gates were closed, water started to cover ruins.

When this happened, I remembered my feelings about the ancient Lycian city I had seen decades ago at Kekova and wrote the poem 'A Boat On The House', dedicating it to Allianoi. So, while the poem is about Kekova, I dedicated the poem to Allianoi."

[30] Aytül Akal says this about her poem, 'The Mountain and the Sea', which was also originally published in Turkish in the book, *Denizin Büyüsü*:
"The Earth is gradually changing and while it does, so do we.

With this poem, I wanted to express the idea that everything on Earth is connected and is constantly influencing each other: In fact ALL IS ONE!

The huge mountain that we think will be there forever actually turns into sand and slips into the sea by erosion. And the sea, by movement of the earth surface, may gradually turn into a mountain. All these huge changes we may not be aware of, however change is and always will be there.

In fact I believe evolutions and improvements are possible only with changes. Therefore, I tried to express the love of a mountain for the sea, and of the sea for the mountain, to emphasize that love makes people ONE and we should be tolerant of each other, as I am you and you are me."

[31] 'Questions to the Rock', jointly written by Aytül Akal and Mavisel Yener, was originally published in Turkish in the book, *Kaç Güneş Var?*
Aytül Akal tells us this about 'Questions to the Rock': "About a decade ago, Mavisel Yener and myself were invited to Cologne, Germany, for an event.

After the presentations, we found time to go around the city, and while visiting the Historic Old Town, we imagined the people who had lived there in the past and who perhaps thought their life would never end. So much desire for glory and prosperity during such a short stay on the Earth! And so much harm done, to satisfy human greed! The rocks used in constructing ancient buildings were surely guardians of many stories about many people.

Then we thought about the rocks found in nature anywhere on the Earth, which have survived many centuries and witnessed so many stories... So we shared our questions with an imaginary rock.

We always write poems wherever we are. We also wrote a poem about the moon which seemed to rise three times that afternoon! (As we moved around, the moon appeared again and again from several aspects!)

So you see, no matter how old we are, we are still children, forever full of poems..."

POETRY PUBLISHED BY PROVERSE

Bliss of Bewilderment, by Birgit Bunzel Linder.
(scheduled) 2017.

Chasing Light, by Patricia Glinton Meicholas. 2013.

China Suite and other Poems, by Gillian Bickley. 2009.

For the Record and other Poems of Hong Kong,
by Gillian Bickley, 2003.

Frida Kahlo's Cry and other Poems, by Laura Solomon. 2015.

Home, Away, Elsewhere, by Vaughan Rapatahana. 2011.

Immortelle and Bhandaaraa Poems,
by Lelawattee Manoo-Rahming. 2011.

In Vitro, by Laura Solomon. 2nd ed. 2013.

Irreverent Poems for Pretentious People,
by Henrik Hoeg. 2016.

Moving House and other Poems from Hong Kong,
by Gillian Bickley. 2005.

Of Symbols Misused, by Mary-Jane Newton. March 2011.

Over the Years, by Gillian Bickley. (scheduled) 2017.

Painting the Borrowed House: Poems,
by Kate Rogers. 2008.

Perceptions, by Gillian Bickley. 2012.

Rain on the Pacific Coast, by Elbert Siu Ping Lee. 2013.

refrain, by Jason S. Polley. 2010.

Shadow Play, by James Norcliffe. 2012.

Shadows in Deferment, by Birgit Bunzel Linder. 2013.

Shifting Sands, by Deepa Vanjani. 2016.

Sightings: a collection of poetry, with an essay, 'communicating poems', by Gillian Bickley. 2007.

Smoked pearl: Poems of Hong Kong and Beyond,
by Akin Jeje (Akinsola Olufemi Jeje). 2010.

The Burning Lake, by Jonathan Locke Hart. November 2016.

Unlocking, by Mary-Jane Newton. 2013.

Wonder, Lust & Itchy feet, by Sally Dellow. 2011.

POETRY – CHINESE LANGUAGE

For the record and other poems of Hong Kong,
by Gillian Bickley. Translated by Simon Chow. 2010. E-bk.

Moving House and other poems from Hong Kong, translated into Chinese, with additional material,
by Gillian Bickley. Edited by Tony Ming-Tak Yip. Translated by Tony Yip & others. 2008.

~~~

FIND OUT MORE ABOUT OUR AUTHORS, BOOKS, EVENTS AND INTERNATIONAL PRIZES

Visit our website
http://www.proversepublishing.com

Visit our distributor's website
<www.chineseupress.com>

Follow us on Twitter
Follow news and conversation: <twitter.com/Proversebooks>
OR
Copy and paste the following to your browser window and
follow the instructions: https://twitter.com/#!/ProverseBooks

"Like" us on www.facebook.com/ProversePress

Request our E-Newsletter
Send your request to info@proversepublishing.com.

Availability
Most titles are available in Hong Kong and world-wide
from our Hong Kong-based Distributor,
The Chinese University Press of Hong Kong,
The Chinese University of Hong Kong, Shatin, NT,
Hong Kong SAR, China. Web: chineseupress.com

All titles are available from Proverse Hong Kong
and the Proverse Hong Kong UK-based Distributor.

We have stock-holding retailers in Hong Kong,
Singapore (Select Books),
Canada (Elizabeth Campbell Books),
Principality of Andorra (Llibreria La Puça, La Llibreria).

Orders can be made from bookshops in the UK and elsewhere.

Ebooks
Most of our titles are available also as Ebooks.